Liturgical Language and Translation:

The Issues Arising from the Revised English Translation of the Roman Missal

Edited by

Thomas O'Loughlin

Professor of Historical Theology, University of Nottingham

D1595635

The cover picture shows a comparison between the 1973 and the 2011 translations of the latin text.

First published May 2014
© The Editors and contributors 2014
ISSN: 0951-2667
ISBN: 978-4-84825-625-5

Contents

The Contributors

John Ball is a Mill Hill Missionary currently teaching sixth-form Philosophy of Religion in a North London secondary school.

Paul F. Bradshaw is Professor of Liturgy at the University of Notre Dame, Indiana.

Juliette Day is a Lecturer in Theology at the University of Helsinki and an editor of *Anaphora*.

Thomas O'Loughlin is Professor of Historical Theology at the University of Nottingham.

Patricia Rumsey is a Poor Clare nun and a lecturer in liturgy at Sarum College, Wiltshire.

Janet E. Rutherford is a patrologist and liturgist living in the Diocese of Meath and an Honorary Lecturer at the University of Nottingham.

Thomas R. Whelan is Associate Professor of Theology at the Milltown Institute, Dublin and had links with ICEL from 1982 until 2003.

Introduction

During last year's miserable spring, a friend teaching English as a foreign language in Dublin – *note the location* – told me this story. Seeking to encourage her students to converse with native speakers, she suggested they use the bad weather as an opening gambit to engage those sitting with them on the bus in conversation. The following day she enquired how they had got on. One student burst into tears saying that the Irish are too unfriendly, indeed too rude, to talk! The teacher asked what happened. The student had said to the man next to her on the bus: 'Aren't we having awful weather?' He replied: 'Don't talk to me!' Here the conversation ended, and the student was so offended that she got off the bus and cried. Why are Dubliners so rude?

In this story, in print, you have no guide to the tone used, where the emphasis fell, nor any hint about facial or bodily expression as the man said: 'Don't talk to me!' But perhaps it is even more complex. If this learner of English had said what she did in London, the reply would have been: 'Tell me about it!' (to which the response is not 'and which aspect should I tell you about?'). In fact, if for some reason one wished to record such a conversation in Latin, the response would be rendered by a single word: '*etiam!*' (that is, if Latin still had a colloquial register). But the story illustrates a fundamental aspect of language: it belongs to the world in which we live, it belongs to our communication with one another in a community, it is rich in meanings quite apart from what can be conveyed in writing, and it is personal. The fact that the Dubliner said what he did shows that he was at ease in the conversation and (however bizarre it might seem to someone not from the banks of the Liffey) that he actually was willing to talk to the student. Language is, after all, *our language*: it belongs to those who use it and is as peculiar to them as any other aspect of their culture. In a world with global technology for communication, it is easy to forget that language has its origin in conversation and communication face to face. Indeed, the debacle over the 2011 translation of the *Missale Romanum* will have served a useful purpose if it reminds us of this aspect of how we talk, communicate and pray.

This new translation did not appear out of a blue sky. By the late 1990s it was clear that a new agenda with regard to the liturgy was abroad within the structures of the Roman Catholic Church.[1] This 'Restorationist' party were, however, faced with a dilemma. On the one hand, they had deep regrets over the whole project of liturgical reform which many had only engaged with on a minimalist basis using a strategy which became known as 'the hermeneutic of continuity'.[2] On the other hand, Paul VI's missal had been mandated by a council and lawfully promulgated: it therefore demanded assent and obedience as authoritative. They could not just 'chuck it' without finding themselves classed with the very people they sought to punish for lesser acts of disobedience. The dilemma's exit seemed to lie with language: translate the liturgical texts so that they side-lined the dynamic of liturgical evolution that had been at work within the Roman Catholic Church since the mid-1950s, if not even earlier.[3] This new strategy resulted in the 2001 'instruction' *Liturgiam authenticam* (LA).[4]

The strategy concerned is well exposed by Jeffery's 2005 book, *Translating Tradition: A Chant Historian Reads* Liturgiam authenticam. Although it provoked reaction from some liturgists for its non-traditional view of liturgical language, it is mandatory reading for anyone engaging with translation questions: Jeffery demonstrates not only how LA breaks with tradition but is internally contradictory[5] – and underlines the dangers involved, because it would jeopardize ecumenical endeavours.[6] But liturgists apart, this document went largely unnoticed at the time. It was only when the translation of the Latin texts appeared in 2011 that it began to generate widespread concern. The letters' columns of periodicals, such as *The Tablet*, began to have a steady stream of

---

[1] See Marini (2007) for an overview; while Taylor (2009), 35–74 gives the detail.
[2] This had been identified as early as 1967 by Karl Rahner: see Rahner and Häussling (1968), 7–9.
[3] See Bugnini (1990); and for the larger context: Fenwick and Spinks (1995).
[4] It can be found on the Vatican website and is printed in Jeffery (2005), 123–65.
[5] Jeffery (2005) – originally a series of articles in Worship.
[6] See Allen (2001); Johnson (2006) and (2007).

complaints about the problematic idiom, the lack of clarity, the difficulties of enunciation, the absence of consultation and the rifts it created ecumenically. In reply, there came only the repeated assurance that it was 'more faithful to the Latin' as if that were not only a liturgical good in itself, but the highest commendation any text could achieve. 'Faithfulness to the Latin' meant, it was argued, automatically that the resulting liturgy would be an improvement on what had gone before![7] Moreover, many bishops around the world entered the debate loud in the new translation's praise – invariably claiming this because they had checked its fidelity to the Latin or to the most recent instruction on translating – while also assuring all that a little more use would bring familiarity and contentment.

However, in the autumn of 2011 a handful of liturgists, an even mix of Catholics and Anglicans, encouraged by a lively debate at the Catholic Theological Association of Great Britain's annual conference felt that some deeper issues needed to be explored and organized a study day on the topic in the Spring of 2012.[8] The papers were considered to be of such relevance to widespread concerns that Professor Michael Hayes, editor of *The Pastoral Review*, asked to publish them; and they appeared *seriatim* in late 2012 and early 2013.[9] However, the din of criticism of the new translation did not die down but has steadily increased: there are now widespread feelings of alienation from the liturgy, which the translation has generated. Indeed, recently the semi-official publication of the Irish Episcopal Commission for Liturgy contained this statement about the new translation:

> Its merits and demerits are well known. It is a fuller and more literal translation but its style often has an awkwardness that in many cases can be overcome by careful preparation – a very good thing in itself. A review is promised, though the mechanism of such a review is not known.

---

[7] See O'Loughlin (2012a).
[8] I wish to thank The Tablet Trust for a grant that made that study day possible.
[9] I wish to thank him for his support and permission to re-publish them.

However, such a review is necessary if we are to listen to what is being said and what is happening, the scholarly and pastoral criticism of the translation and the instruction on translation but also including its non-acceptance by some, the use of a mixture of old and new translations by others and the disturbing quietness of congregations to the new responses and other parts.[10]

This is about as close as anyone with a formal connection to any Episcopal Conference has come to admitting that not only is the translation a failure, but that *Liturgiam authenticam* is wrong-headed.

In view of the continuing interest in the problem and the promise of a review in the future, we thought it would be good to bring these papers, further up-dated in some cases, into one convenient location – and are grateful to the Alcuin/GROW series of Joint Liturgical Studies for providing the ideal vehicle for a publication of this size. We hope that these essays will help all involved in studying the issue of translating the Roman Rite into a modern language. Moreover, we all wrote conscious that these issues cannot today be discussed as if other churches do not exist – our liturgies have grown too alike for that – and so this is an ecumenical concern of primary importance. Lastly, the issue of language is, at the moment, particularly troubling to English-speaking Roman Catholics, but the questions around language and how it is used and functions in liturgy are never far away from worshippers, and we hope that these papers, occasioned by specific situation, may also throw light on the larger and wider issue.

We might all remind ourselves of what Bede said regarding the beauty of a piece of English poetry, Caedmon's hymn, in contrast to the poverty of his own Latin translation of it: '*ex alia in aliam linguam ad verbum sine detrimento sui decoris ac dignitatis transferri*'.[11]

---

[10] Jones (2013), 9.

[11] Bede, *Historia ecclesiastica gentis Anglorum* 4,24: 'one cannot translate, word for word, from one tongue to another without loss of elegance and dignity'.

1

Liturgical Translation and Participation

Thomas R. Whelan

In 1965, addressing a gathering of those involved in the task of translating liturgical text into the vernacular, Pope Paul VI used the well-known words of St Jerome to describe the virtual impossibility of their task:

> If I translate word for word, it sounds absurd; if I am forced to change something in the word order or style, I seem to have stopped being a translator.[1]

That is how St Jerome describes the dilemma. When a *verbatim* account of a text into a second language is not possible, we are forced to become hermeneuts: for the sake of comprehension or in order to respect the integrity of a receptor language, we are required to *interpret* the original text. Herein lies the problem, one which *Liturgiam authenticam* (LA) of 2001[2] seems to acknowledge in some of its prescriptions but which was not fully respected in the received text of the new translation into English of the *Missale Romanum* of 2008.

Translation Procedures

The history of translation is one of tension between giving priority to the original language or to the target language. And the debate continues today. LA chose to give an unquestioned priority to the original Latin text. While not beyond criticism, this can be justified when one considers that the

---

[1] Full text in ICEL (1982), n. 786.
[2] See Jeffery (2005), 121–65 for full text.

Liturgy Constitution itself (SC) gives to the Latin language 'a privileged character as the official language of the Roman liturgy'.[3] We have been given Latin text to translate and must deal with this in a most responsible way. While respecting the integrity of the original and its function as prayer, the translated texts must be capable of facilitating people in their encounter with God. [4]

Like many Roman documents, there seem to be (at least) two different people drafting the text of LA. On the one hand, some of the stipulations show an appreciation of the difficulties inherent in translating into a receptor language. An instance of this is found in LA 25:

> So that the content of the original texts may be evident and comprehensive even to the faithful who lack any special intellectual formation, the translations should be characterized by a kind of language which is easily understandable, yet which at the same time preserves these texts' dignity, beauty, and doctrinal precision.

Other principles reflect this concern to retain the balance between fidelity to the Latin and the accomplishment of what is, fundamentally, the purpose of any translation: communication of an original text into a receptor or target language, so that those dependent on the target language might be able to enter, however imperfectly, into an understanding of the original (e.g., LA 20, 28, 53, 59). The fact that the permissive phrase *quantum fieri potest* ('insofar as possible') is found some 17 times throughout the document is an implicit acknowledgement that good translation is an almost impossible task because choices need to be made.

On the other hand there are principles in LA limiting any attempt to respect the genius of the receptor language. For instance, some sections restrict the employment of genderized language (30–31); or require the

---

[3] Collins (1990), 652.
[4] See ICEL (1982), n. 880. Another discussion which cannot be taken up here, and one that remains possible in current Roman procedures, is the creation of new texts which respect the genius of the English language, along the lines encouraged by no. 43 of the Instruction from the Consilium, Comme le prévoit, which guided all translation work from 1969 until the publication of LA.)

use of capitalization where it occurs in the Latin – even when the Latin usage does not correspond to what is accepted practice in a target language (33); or expect that translated terms of key Latin vocabulary follow what is found in the 'authoritative vernacular translation of the Catechism of the Catholic Church' (50a).

The stated goal of the process instigated by LA (2001) seems to be the contribution 'to the gradual development, in each vernacular, of a sacred style that will come to be recognized as proper to liturgical language' (27; see 47). To this end the various subordinate and relative clauses, the ordering of words and other stylistic features particular to the Latin language need to be maintained 'as completely as possible' (57a; see 47 and 59). The overseeing influence of the Roman agency for English language translation, *Vox Clara*, meant that many of the final texts of ICEL 2008 (the one which received the canonical approval of various Episcopal Conferences) were modified in a way that seems to have ignored the moderating influence of some of the prescriptions of LA. *Vox Clara's* final version of 2011 offers some extreme examples of that to which 'formal equivalence' is supposed to refer, in that it is unhelpfully literalist in how it occasionally gives an unreasonable priority to the original language even in matters that do not relate to the deposit of faith. At times it bears witness to modifications made by people who, it seems, had no understanding of the rather complex task that is translation, who did not always respect the grammatical subtleties of the Latin original the integrity of which they purported to protect and who often did not understand how good literate English operates, either syntactically or functionally. The capacity to speak English does not always imply the capacity to write good literary text, even less, to translate for public proclamation. The oral and aural qualities of language which are *intrinsic* to liturgical prayer and its proclamation were all but ignored. Probably one of the more serious lacunae in the new translation is that the inner sense of language is not always respected.

Participation in Liturgy

While SC permitted a rather limited use of vernacular in the liturgy, the movement throughout the world towards its more generous application was such that, by the time the first Latin edition of the Missal appeared in 1970, it was presumed that texts would be translated so as to facilitate greater comprehension of the liturgy and thereby better participation. We need to recall that 'full, active and conscious participation' in the liturgy (SC 14) was the first principle of liturgical reform set out in the SC to guide its work of pastoral renewal. From the 1980s onwards, a realization began to emerge that 'participation' meant something more than 'liturgical activism'. External forms of participation give expression to and serve the creation of a deeper interior engagement with the mystery of God being celebrated, finding, ultimately, its source in Trinitarian participation. A recent posthumous publication of the British-born American liturgical scholar, Mark Searle, speaks of three levels of participation: participation through ritual behaviour; participation through liturgy in the ecclesial body of Christ and participation in the life of God.[5]

Reflection on the formative and mystagogical objectives of participation encouraged scholars to revisit the idea of 'comprehension' in liturgy as well as to consider the dynamics that come into play when we speak of 'understanding' in prayer text. Comprehension in liturgy is something more than simply a cognitive activity. It refers to the deepening of our encounter, as assembly, with the Triune God in and through the paschal mystery of Christ. It could be said that the formation that takes place in liturgy is grounded, in the first place, in the very *fact* of the liturgical event, before it lodged in prayer text.[6] If the ritual complexity of the liturgy supplies the context of our verbal prayer, then we need to realize that ritual of its nature is ambivalent and therefore always beyond our total comprehension. The ritual dimension of Christian worship, because it helps shape the environment for an encounter with God through paschal mystery in the Spirit, cannot ever be fully grasped until these last times, the *eschaton*, find their fulfilment in the second *parousia* of Christ in glory.

Comprehension in Liturgy

A number of references in SC point to the importance of the capacity of

---

[5] See Searle (2006)
6 See Whelan (2008).

the reformed rites and texts to be easily understood by the worshipping assembly in view of its being able to assume a rightful 'full, active and conscious participation' in the sacred action. SC 11 directs that the faithful take part *'fully aware of what they are doing,* actively engaged in the rite and enriched by its effects'; SC 21, that the reformed rites be *'understood with ease';* and that the rites, now 'short, clear and unencumbered by useless repetitions', should *'be within the people's power of comprehension'* (SC 34). The successful implementation of these directives was deemed, by many people, to be of the essence of what makes 'good liturgy'. Unfortunately, as a pastoral principle, this criterion has been shaped by a rather dubious reading of how liturgy functions.

If the aspiration to reform the liturgy so as to facilitate 'full, active and conscious participation' is worthy, then we must admit in hindsight that the means to achieve this were presented with a certain naivety. The insights of ritual studies, which only began to emerge a decade after SC was promulgated, were not available to the framers of the Liturgy Constitution. One would concur with the comment of Aidan Kavanagh when he says that SC 34 offers 'an educationalist outlook, certainly not that of anyone knowing anything about ritual behaviour, which is rarely short, clear, free of repetition and usually transcends the comprehension of the whole congregation, including its officiants'. As a result, the post-Vatican II liturgy, in the hands of insensitive presiders and ministers, becomes an experience of 'aggressive educationalism when used imprudently'.[7]

The perspective found in SC 11, 21 and 34 often 'assumed a univocal, pre-critical, common-sense notion of the nature' of communication and how this operates.[8] There seems to have been no sense that, not only are symbol, gesture and rite equivocal, but so also is language. This is one of the faulty understandings of language in LA, which requires at times fidelity in translation to the words and syntactical structure of Latin that does not, in its striving after literalism, respect the translation process.

---

7 Kavanagh, (1998), 449.
8 See Collins (1990), 655.

Faith Context for Comprehension

Liturgy is first of all about a Spirit-driven encounter with the Triune God through the paschal event of Christ before it is about anything else. The capacity to understand what takes place in liturgy, as well as to facilitate an appropriate ease with participation, is helped by translation into the vernacular. But this by itself does not necessarily mean that texts will be understood. Good proclamation of liturgical prayers is important, but not sufficient. Presiders must be people who are equal to their task, who are capable of proclaiming and who have developed in themselves, as leaders of the assembly, a sense of how to pray in public, of how to inhabit the text, of how to use language as a ritual component in the very complex and multi-layered communicative act that, at the end of the day, transacts with salvation in the midst of the assembly.

The celebration of liturgy requires at least a minimal faith context before any sort of meaningful engagement can take place. However, liturgy is *not*, in the first place, a catechetical tool; nor is it, in the first place, the arena for mission. This implies, nonetheless, the need for a catechetical dimension, which, almost by definition, has to be pre-liturgical (at least, in the formal sense).

Rather, 'understanding' requires of people, firstly, that they are deeply involved in the liturgy as a *faith experience* and engaged with one another and with God. 'Meaning' in prayers will be in direct proportion to the relationship between the content of the prayer and the religious experience of believers of which prayer is an expression. Liturgical prayers need not only be understood as an exercise of the mind, but also appropriated as religious experience of the heart. In order, therefore, that 'understanding' might take place, the literary text proclaimed in the assembly needs to be capable, through its qualities of orality and aurality, of being accessed at a level below that of the surface level. Hence the need for good text.

A basic level of intelligibility is a requirement of the prayer of the assembly. But the translated texts only function in the context of the living ecclesial faith of those who employ it. The assembly locates and then validates the intelligibility of a prayer text ultimately in its collective memory of the salvific workings of a Triune God, revealed in biblical narrative as well as through its own individual faith memory.

Liturgical language has the power to offer to the assembly an echo of its own story, the story of its salvation history which binds it together and to God, in Christ. It can be capable of becoming a means of giving expression to the religious experience of the ecclesial community. The assembly as it gathers to do its dominical thing each week on the Lord's Day must already have a minimum level of access to the biblical, ritual, symbolic and literary genres that converge to create of this ritual gathering, a Christian liturgy.

Conclusion

As early as 1981 ICEL had recognized the inadequacy of its 1973 missal translation, and it embarked upon a long and carefully planned project to revise its translated work. The necessary resources were put in place and the experience of over 20 years of praying in the vernacular was appealed to, along with a wide consultation through the bishops of its 11 full-member Episcopal Conferences. The revised text of the missal was completed and sent to Rome by these Conferences in 1998, only to be rejected a number of years later, without explanation.

The translation needed to be done. The English language *Roman Missal* of 2011 is far from representing our best effort. It does have some wonderful moments, and its attempts at a new syntactic style are to be welcomed, but it also has a large number of awkward English constructions not native to the language, some bad grammar and not a few horrendous texts that make it challenging, to say the least, to speak publicly.

Ultimately, any liturgy we celebrate must facilitate an encounter with God and lead towards transformation in our own lives, in the lives of the liturgical assembly, as well as in the society to which we belong. If liturgy does not lead us to bear witness to the transformative power of the paschal mystery, which continues to operate until the end of time, then our liturgical worship, in any language, is in vain.

2

Ecumenical Participation in Liturgical Translation

Paul F. Bradshaw

Right from the start of work on translating into English the new liturgical texts emanating from the Second Vatican Council there was an ecumenical dimension to the enterprise. Even before the International Commission on English in the Liturgy (ICEL) was established in the autumn of 1965, representatives of the Roman Catholic Liturgical Commission for England and Wales had attended meetings of the Church of England Liturgical Commission and *vice versa*. Preliminary drafts of such texts as the Creeds, the *Gloria in excelsis* and the Lord's Prayer were shared with the Church of England Commission.[1] Later, in 1966, the appointment of ecumenical observers at the Concilium Liturgicum in Rome facilitated more ecumenical contacts, and those observers attended meetings of ICEL's Advisory Committee, which were usually held in conjunction with those of the Concilium. It was here that the International Consultation on English Texts (ICET), an ecumenical forum complementary to ICEL's work, came into being, and through its membership links were established to Joint Liturgical Group of Great Britain, an ecumenical body with representatives from all the main churches in the country (except at first the Roman Catholic Church), set up in 1963 and already engaged in producing material that might be adopted in its member churches. In the USA there were similar links to the Consultation on Common Texts, another ecumenical body set

---

[1] See Jasper (1989), 288.

up in 1969 to develop in conjunction with ICET agreed versions of liturgical material that might be used in common by various churches.

The aim of this cooperation between the Roman Catholic ICEL and the ecumenical ICET was to produce agreed versions of commonly used liturgical texts said or sung by the congregation (as distinct from presidential prayers) that might be adopted in as many churches as possible in the English-speaking world. The first phase of their work resulted in the publication in 1970 of *Prayers We Have in Common*, which was enlarged and revised in the following year and then appeared in a second revised edition in 1975.[2] This version included the Lord's Prayer, the Apostles' and Nicene Creeds, *Kyrie, Gloria in excelsis, Sursum corda, Sanctus* and *Benedictus, Agnus Dei, Gloria Patri* and the canticles *Benedictus, Te Deum laudamus, Magnificat* and *Nunc dimittis*.

In 1983 at a congress of Societas Liturgica held in Vienna, it was agreed to convene a new organization similar in ecumenical purpose to ICET but with a more clearly defined membership and with broader goals of ecumenical liturgical collaboration, and so two years later at the next congress of Societas Liturgica in Boston, Massachusetts, the successor to ICET was formally established – the English Language Liturgical Consultation, ELLC. The ordinary membership of ELLC was to be the national or regional associations in which the respective churches or their liturgical committees or commissions came together on an ecumenical basis. These national or regional associations appoint or otherwise designate their representatives on ELLC and include within their membership churches of the Anglican, Lutheran, Methodist, Reformed, Roman Catholic and United traditions, but are also open to the Orthodox and other Eastern churches and to other Christian traditions such as the Free Churches.

The first major project of ELLC was completed in 1988 with the publication of a revised version of *Prayers we have in Common* called *Praying Together*, based upon ICET's earlier work.[3] Other parts of its activities have included gathering and studying Eucharistic Prayers of

---

[2] ICET (1970 and 1975)
[3] ELLC (1988); and (1990).

common interest, the promotion of *The Revised Common Lectionary* prepared by the North American Consultation on Common Texts and surveys of member associations and through them, their parent churches about liturgical developments, so as to provide a common forum for the exchange of information.

Many of the texts in *Praying Together* were incorporated into their liturgical books by a number of churches throughout the English-speaking world. The one that caused the most difficulties, however, was the Lord's Prayer, and above all the line previously translated as 'lead us not into temptation'. ICET at first rendered it as 'Do not bring us to the test'. The accompanying commentary observed:

> Two errors must be avoided in this line. The first is the misconception that God can be the agent of temptation: the second is that the original Greek word means 'temptation' as it is meant today. The reference here is primarily eschatological. It is probably a petition for deliverance from the final "time of trial" which, in biblical thought, marks the Last Days and the full revelation of anti-Christ... Yet a reference to any occasion of testing, when issues of life and death are in the balance, is not excluded. Either way, it is certainly not subjective moral temptations that are basically envisaged.[4]

In spite of this explanation, this particular prayer was simply too well known and deeply loved in its more traditional version for this newer, if more accurate, rendering to be easily acceptable to many Christians. Of all the liturgical texts in the collection, therefore, it was the one that was most often rejected by churches, or alternatively only adopted with some emendation. Thus, for example, this particular line was altered in the Church of England's 1973 experimental rite, Series 3, to 'Do not bring us to the time of trial'. Even though ICET subsequently amended

---

[4] ICET (1970), 7–8. This observation was reproduced with minor variations in later editions of the texts.

their translation to 'Save us from the time of trial', in the end neither of these renderings proved acceptable to the General Synod of the Church of England, which restored the familiar 'Lead us not into temptation' in both its 1980 *Alternative Service Book* and its 2000 *Common Worship* volume, although also printing in the latter the ecumenical version elsewhere in a section of 'Prayers for Various Occasions', with a note permitting its use 'on suitable occasions'.

Even the ICET version of the Nicene Creed ran into problems in the Church of England. Although ICET had originally translated the line concerning Christ's incarnation as 'by the power of the Holy Spirit he was born of the Virgin Mary and became man', in its second revised edition of 1975 this became 'by the power of the Holy Spirit he became incarnate from the Virgin Mary and was made man'. It was the preposition 'from' that troubled some members of the General Synod and led to a reversion to 'of' in the 1980 book. In a bizarre twist, after ELLC in its 1990 revision of the texts adopted instead 'was incarnate of the Holy Spirit and the Virgin Mary and became truly human', the General Synod voted for 'was incarnate from the Holy Spirit and the Virgin Mary and was made man'!

The major turning-point in ecumenical liturgical cooperation came in 2001 with the publication of the Vatican Instruction, *Liturgiam Authenticam*,[5] which mandated that a more literal rather than dynamically equivalent approach to the translation of Latin liturgical texts into vernacular languages be adopted. Such a decision obviously would affect the ecumenical translation work that had been done over nearly 40 years. That such a consequence was not merely unintended collateral damage, however, is revealed by the Instruction itself, when it stated that in the process of translation, 'great caution is to be taken to avoid a wording or style that the Catholic faithful would confuse with the manner of speech of non-Catholic ecclesial communities or of other religions, so that such a factor will not cause them confusion or discomfort' (n. 40). In other words, one of the principles of any new translations in the Roman Catholic Church was that they should deliberately be different from whatever other Christians were using. There is, however, a supreme irony in this, as my

---

[5] See Jefffery (2005), 123–65.

colleague Maxwell Johnson has pointed out with such clarity. He observes with regard to English translations that the expression 'the manner of speech of non-Catholic ecclesial communities' can only be referring to the common texts produced by ICET and ELLC, and he continues:

> [T]hese very texts in their earlier form appeared in the approved English translation of the Missal of Paul VI in 1970 and in subsequent editions. *The Lutheran Book of Worship*, which employs the similar texts, did not appear until 1978, and Rite II of the American Episcopal *Book of Common Prayer*, published in 1979, also uses comparable texts. Other churches prepared their worship books either at the same time or subsequent to these publications. That is, 'the manner of speech of non-Catholic ecclesial communities' in their liturgical language is based directly on the manner of *Catholic* liturgical speech because it is adapted directly *from* already existing Catholic liturgical speech! It is not and simply could not have been the other way around, even if for Roman Catholics ecumenical consultation had been a part of the process. Of course, this will now become self-fulfilling since the only Christian Churches using the former ICEL texts will be those in the English-speaking Protestant world. Ironically, then, the former Roman Catholic ICEL texts *will* now become the 'manner of [liturgical] speech of non-Catholic ecclesial communities' alone.[6]

There is an even greater irony than that, as Max Johnson goes on to point out. The 'new' translations produced in the Roman Catholic Church in some ways bear an uncanny resemblance to the English translations of the missal that were produced for the edification of the faithful in the years prior to the Second Vatican Council, even though they were not

---

[6] Johnson (2007), 56–7 (italics in original).

used liturgically; and those translations had tended to adopt the style and vocabulary of the Anglican and Lutheran churches of the time.[7] So, the Roman Catholic Church today uses English texts that resemble what 'non-Catholic ecclesial communities' once used to use, and those communities today use texts based on what the Roman Catholic Church adopted after the Second Vatican Council. Curioser and curioser, as Alice might have said.

Rather oddly, *Liturgiam authenticam* itself did seem to envisage some continuing consultation with other churches. It stated: 'With due regard for Catholic traditions and for all of the principles and norms contained in this Instruction, an appropriate relationship or coordination is greatly to be desired, whenever possible, between any translations intended for common use in the various Rites of the Catholic Church' (n. 90); and went on to say that 'a similar agreement is desirable with the particular non-Catholic Eastern churches or with the authorities of the Protestant ecclesial communities, provided that it is not a question of a liturgical text pertaining to doctrinal matters still in dispute, and provided also that the Churches or ecclesial communities involved have a sufficient number of adherents and that those consulted are truly capable of functioning as representatives of the same ecclesial communities' (n. 91). This looks rather like a direct rejection of working through ELLC, and indeed ICEL was forced to withdraw from ELLC following the publication of *Liturgiam authenticam* because of the latter's proscription on involvement with ecumenical bodies.

With regard to this, Presbyterian ecumenist and liturgist Horace Allen of Boston University has commented:

> The politics of this document are quite obvious. The emphasis on required Vatican approval, the insistence on decisions by conferences of bishops, as opposed to the International Commission on English in the Liturgy, and the dismissive references to 'Protestant ecclesial communities' and their representatives is clear. It signals

---

[7] Johnson (2007), 61–2.

the effective termination of the longstanding international partnership between the Catholic International Commission on English in the Liturgy on the one hand, and the Consultation on Common Texts and the English Language Liturgical Consultation on the other. Toward the end of this sad reversal of many years of happy and fruitful ecumenical collaboration, it is stated with what must be an extraordinarily sardonic note, 'From the day on which this instruction is published, a new period begins for the liturgical use of vernacular language.'[8]

Nonetheless, since then, ELLC has continued to maintain formal and informal contacts with the Pontifical Council for the Promoting of Christian Unity, with the Congregation for Divine Worship, and has even exchanged information with ICEL itself. And in spite of the loss of its principal ecumenical partner, it has continued to meet and pursue its goals. Indeed, out of its 2011 meeting in Reims, France, it issued a statement, *Praying with One Voice*, that outlined its position. On common texts, it said:

> For the first time in history, Christians in the English speaking world are using common liturgical texts. In the process of coming to agreed common texts, scholars from different Christian traditions agreed on principles for the translation from the earliest sources. This in itself has been a gift. Despite only having been in existence for a relatively short time, these texts have been adopted freely by an ever increasing number of churches. We celebrate this. They are being experienced as a gift, a sign and a way to Christian unity in our diversity. As the churches continue to discover the riches of these shared texts, we believe further revision

---

[8] Allen (2001).

is inappropriate at the present time. We invite all who have not yet explored these texts, and those who have departed from their use, to join us in prayerful reflection on the value of common texts and careful consideration of the texts themselves. Prayed together, shared common texts become a part of the fabric of our being. They unite the hearts of Christians in giving glory to God as we undertake the mission of the Gospel.

We encourage

- ongoing creation of resources for ecumenical and liturgical formation through praying common texts
- furthering of scholarship which is faithful to tradition whilst seeking a language which is inclusive and just
- continuing ecumenical reflection on core symbolic actions and gestures, the ordo and shape of liturgy.

All this, however, still leaves me with one major unanswered question. Why did the Roman Catholic Church never follow up on the consultation over translations directly with 'the authorities of the Protestant ecclesial communities' that was proposed in *Liturgiam authenticam* but simply went ahead with its own work? It is true that those bodies might have been reluctant to abandon the texts they had only recently adopted in order to engage in a major round of discussion about re-translation, but nevertheless a significant ecumenical opportunity was then sadly lost.

3
Liturgical Language and the Liturgical Text

Juliette Day

Discussing liturgical worship as a textual activity arouses sensitivity among liturgists as well as worshippers who wish to prioritize ritual and communal activity over an inert text; however, the liturgical text not only determines the words of worship but also our actions and attitudes during worship. In what follows I will explore some of the ways in which the textuality of liturgy affects the way we worship, not just the words of worship by looking first at what language does in worship, then at how the specific context of liturgical worship determines language choices and finally at the nature of the liturgical text.

What does language do in worship?

Language is for communication in worship, just as it is in other areas of life: worshippers communicate with each other, to God, and there is an assumption that God also communicates with them. Such features as dialogues between participants, direct address to the people and the 'Word of the Lord' proclaimed in the readings make that clear. Communication is, though, about meaning and not simply words; the words are just a particular way of communicating. To emphasize the meaning over the choice of words indicates their other task enabling the instruction, edification and transformation of worshippers as members of the body and heirs of the kingdom. Such a task for the liturgical text does not inevitably presume a simplistic liturgical language, but it does require that the meaning is potentially accessible to worshippers, that obfuscation and obscurantism should be avoided.

Often in recent debates one discerns confusion between the complexity of language and the complexity of meaning which the language conveys. If the language is not immediately accessible, then worshippers, of whatever level of education and linguistic skill, will be required to unpack the sentence before unpacking the meaning: that is, they have to translate it just as if it were in a foreign language. This is not just a pastoral issue but also a theological one. Christ conveyed complex ideas, the meaning of which appears to be difficult to unravel as the mountain of New Testament scholarship attests, but did so using the images and language of everyday – someone keeping pigs, looking for something valuable that has been lost, lighting a lamp and then blocking out its light, and, of course, leaving to the church as a memorial of his passion the ordinary stuff of bread and wine. Thus it should be of no surprise to theologians that the everyday can convey the things of the greatest significance and complexity.

Liturgical texts contain theological presuppositions about God, about humanity, about the ordering of creation, about the relationship between people, and between people and God. During worship we restate what sort of God it is that we serve. Thus the very common exclamation 'Lord have mercy' is not a hopeful request nor a command, but a pre-fulfilled request made in the knowledge of a merciful God derived from promises in the Gospels and validated by the experience of worshippers. Certain language choices serve to establish the distinctions in the relationship, most obviously by traditionally reserving 'Thee/Thou/Thine' for God after it had fallen out of use between people, or by using epithets for God which are not used of humans or even heavenly beings – 'ineffable', 'almighty', 'immortal', etc. These are assertions rather than descriptions; they re-state for the community what sort of God it is who hears and answer our prayers.

Jean Ladrière referred to this as 'presentification': it makes these things present and operative in the community which speaks them.[1] So when we announce the mystery of Christ, of his life, death and resurrection, the mystery of salvation, we are not merely quoting authoritative statements but bringing into the present, that which was spoken and which happened

---

[1] Ladrière (1973), 50–62.

in the past. And most markedly, when the words of Christ at the Last Supper are repeated, these words receive again the very efficacy which they had when Christ himself used them.

What sort of language does worship need?

If these are some of the functions of language in the liturgy, then what sort of language should we use? The debates have focussed around whether the language of the liturgy constitutes a distinctive form that could be called 'liturgical language' or even 'sacred language', but that ignores how the context of worship controls the language long before stylistic choices come into play.

Liturgical worship asks us to do more varied things with our language than almost any other context I can think of by requiring a very broad range of communication activities each with their own linguistic form and convention. So, ministers or leaders speak alone in addresses to God on behalf of the congregation or on his/her own behalf, or to the congregation, there may be dialogues with the congregation; the congregation as a whole or a single representative may address the minister, or each other or God. The purpose of the communication varies considerably: to praise God, to make requests, to express sorrow or joy, to convey instructions, to tell stories, to state beliefs. Even when the content may change from week to week, texts often follow established patterns (genres) which affect the way the information is presented and the choice of vocabulary; this is most clearly demonstrated by collects or Eucharistic Prayers or certain forms of intercession. Spoken texts can follow prose patterns, but texts intended for singing are often in metre where the music's demand for rhythm and rhyme may override even further normal syntactical conventions. In addition to music, the words may be accompanied by rituals which extend the meaning beyond what the words at face-value indicate; an obvious example of this would be baptism, where the meaning of 'I baptize you in the name of the Father, and of the Son and of the Holy Spirit' can only be completed by a ritual action involving water. This sort of diversity might not be found in an entire day's output of BBC Radio 4, but in churches it is contained within a single worship event.

What sets liturgical language apart from other speech events in our culture is that it is collective speech; it is not the speech of an individual nor of a collection of individuals, but it is the speech of a group. This has two stylistic effects: that in syntax, rhythm and vocabulary it needs to be easily spoken and that the meaning conveyed has the potential to be assented to by worshippers who use words which they have neither chosen nor composed, thereby suspending the subjective and autonomous speech of other cultural and social activities. The liturgy is shared speech and the responsibility for ensuring that this takes place rests not just on the participants, but also on the liturgical composers.

The theologically and ecclesiologically inspired emphasis on the 'full, active and conscious participation' in the liturgy by the people has implications for the comprehensibility and 'speakability' of all liturgical texts, but especially those which the congregation speak. Congregational texts are for choral recitation which, in order to avoid cacophony and barriers to participation, requires attention to rhythm, 'speakability' and opportunities to breathe, even before one attends to the accessibility of the meaning.[2] 'Speakability', here, describes what remains when any barriers to physical speech are removed, that is, avoiding words of five or more syllables, or avoiding the awkward sequences of consonants or sibilants. Choral recitation also works much better when sentences are broken up into short phrases with a regular rhythm and this has an impact on the way such texts are presented in print with often a very idiosyncratic punctuation.

Choral recitation also requires a much flatter intonation than one might use when reading aloud or speaking in other contexts, which is evident regardless of the communication activity. Speakers opt for clarity and corporate seemliness over the expressions of strong emotion or role-playing in scripture readings: thankfully congregations do not 'bewail our manifold sins and wickedness' as the general confession from the *Book of Common Prayer* suggests they ought!

In common with other groups in society, the Church employs 'technical language' either by using certain words or phrases which are not used

---

[2] Crystal and Davy (1969), 149.

27

anywhere else, or by giving a distinctive meaning to ordinary words. Examples include theological terms like 'consubstantial', 'redemption', 'bless', but also ordinary words such as 'bread', 'cup', 'peace'. Additionally there are partially anglicized loan words from languages unfamiliar to the congregation like 'baptize' or 'eucharist', 'presbyter', etc., or even phrases in a foreign language like '*Kyrie eleison*', '*Christe eleison*', '*Kyrie eleison*'. Other 'exclusive' language exists because of the heavy borrowing of imagery and metaphors from biblical texts. These might be used in direct quotations, such as 'Holy, holy, holy', or in a modified form like the institution narrative in the Eucharistic Prayer, or simply allusions. In addition to vocabulary and imagery, worshippers use greetings which would be unusual outside the liturgy: 'The Lord be with you' rather than 'Good Morning' or 'Hello'. And whereas it would not be considered appropriate to say 'hello' to someone several times during a conversation, this liturgical address may be used three times in one service without attracting comment. Liturgical texts, then, employ vocabulary and imagery which is not common in the surrounding culture but is used without comment by worshippers, because it is part of their culture infused by scripture and their own traditions. But is this an indicator of a distinctive language, or simply a style of language belonging to a sub-culture?

The Liturgical Text

What I have discussed so far has taken no account of the way in which the words we use in the liturgy are given to us. Before we speak these words we read them from a printed text; so in what way is language contained in a text different from language that is simply spoken?

Like any other text, a liturgical text is a physical object. It consists of symbols inscribed on a page in meaningful units, presented according to the conventions and technologies of writing and accessed using the technology of reading. Conventions of writing include adherence to formal grammar, complete sentences, the organization of information according to theme and genre, and the way the contents are presented on the page. When the text is before us, the multiple processes by which it was produced are hidden; reading the text is a transaction between the reader and the text alone. The author can exercise no influence on how I interpret the text – neither where I choose to read it, how skilled I am at reading, what other pieces of information I might bring to my interpretation, or how I might connect it to other texts. And we should also note that we normally read texts silently, reading is a non-physical activity; indeed we have so interiorized the symbol system that we do not need to read every letter of every word in order to understand each sentence.

These observations about how we react to texts can be clearly contrasted with the more immediate communication of speech between people. Such communication is momentary – as Walter Ong so memorably puts it, 'When I pronounce the word "permanence", by the time I get to the "-nence", the "perma-" is gone and has to be gone.'[3] It may be disorganized, it may rely on more than words. The speaker can repeat and reinforce the message in response to questions or puzzled looks. Information may not be presented in a logical way: there will be pauses, digressions. If you hear the speaker telling the same story in another context, the story is unlikely to be exactly the same and will differ in presentation and content even though it might be recognizable as the same.

Liturgical worship is an act of communication in which the speech is dictated by a text. Worship *per se* does not require a text but where present, it certainly controls it. The text indicates the start and end of specific acts of prayer through the use of headings or rubrics; it tells us when to stand or kneel, what the priest is to do with his hands at the altar, that we should process to the font; it may recommend that we sing something. Furthermore, even our attitudes and emotional response may be directed by the text – invitations to pray, to confess our sins, to give thanks, to lift up our hearts prepare us to respond appropriately to the textual element which follows. In fact the liturgical text could be compared to a ready cake-mix which contains everything except the participants.

One of the myths which enables us to use liturgical texts is that they contain the words which we would want to use anyway, that worship is essentially an oral experience and that the written text is an afterthought.

---

[3] Ong (2002), 32.

Myths though useful are not usually true – liturgical texts are highly unlikely to have had a pre-textual life, and certainly not translated liturgical texts. They are not words which have been recorded from a speech event, but words provided from a text production process to be spoken aloud. Liturgical worship is very far removed from the speech events of everyday life and from ritual speech in non-literate cultures; it is text-based and text-bound. The authors of liturgical texts use their experience and skills as writers and the technology of text production; readers/worshippers bring to the liturgical text the reading and interpretative strategies they use for all other texts. We do not become different sorts of authors and readers when we enter church or do things with the liturgical text. Note what happens when the Gospel reading is provided for the people on a printed paper – there is a ritual procession to the centre of the church from where we are asked *to listen* to the Holy Gospel so that Christ's words may be proclaimed in the midst of the people, to which the congregation respond by engaging in the interiorized, private and non-physical act of reading the Sunday leaflet. A similar retreat from the communal to the private will occur when following along with the missal, especially when some editions have helpfully provided the Latin as a parallel text.

Conclusion

So I find myself in an ambivalent place with regard to the text. The liturgical text is simply a text, just like any other. The letters and numbers and grammar are the same, the basic skills I need to access the information are the same. We may use our language liturgically, choosing to use words, phrases, genres, etc. that make sense in the context of communal worship, but the language cannot be sacred in itself. The encounter with the living God is beyond the liturgical text, rather it occurs through the activity of a community gathered in his name, as Christ promised. It is the activity of gathering in the presence of God that is sacred, and this happens after and beyond the text, and even after and beyond language.

4

A Liturgy of the Word and the Words of the Liturgy

Thomas O'Loughlin

For us Christians, the communities of the disciples of Jesus, all liturgy must be an encounter with him and his prayer to the Father. This is the *mysterium* constituting our liturgy: it is not a matter of imposed rites performed as a matter of obeying divine commands nor fulfilling the demands of the virtue of religion. This is the reality of *anamnesis* echoing in the words 'do this in memory of me', which encounters the presence of the Father's Anointed among us: it is not a matter of repetitious imitation. This is our re-hearing the Scriptures which, through the Spirit, lead us into the truth: it is neither attention to, nor study of, a set of sacral 'spiritual' texts. Indeed, such is our liturgy's nature that we often describe it as the encounter *hodie* with the One we confess as incarnate: the Christ is the sacrament of our encounter with God; and the encounter's privileged moment is the liturgy. As such, the liturgy takes place within the creation and addresses the Father from the creation: it is must not be seen as an esoteric activity. Over 60 years after Pope Pius XII's encyclical *Mediator Dei*, this view of the liturgy is hardly new; and, indeed it should be a moment of thankfulness for Catholics, that the 'Liturgical Movement' which took official form with Pius and inspired those who worked for the reforms of Vatican II, is now having an influence far beyond the bounds of Catholicism. But if this theological position – the encounter with the liturgy is a moment in the incarnation of the Lord – is widely accepted when we think abstractly of 'liturgy'; does it inform our practice, the actual way we celebrate liturgy?

At the outset, we should recall that it is very easy to change theologies: new books are written, new encyclicals issued, new students arrive, and so the jargon in the classroom changes! But liturgy – because it involves *doing* – is a matter of repetition. Each week we reiterate what happened the previous week, once a pattern of behaviour has been established, the usage of a building, the ingrained habits that act as instruction manuals for sacristans and organists, all tend towards continuity in practice – and an inevitable formalism – that works silently against change. This is the phenomenon of stasis that allows historians to see how liturgies drifted apart and retained elements (often with heightened 'sacral' effect, following a rule of thumb that, if I do not understand it, its rationale must be very 'deep') that no longer made sense. The 'sweeping' of the corporal for crumbs, for example, that occurred at low mass until 1969, despite the fact that those crumbs had ceased to be a problem around 1000 years ago when the western churches began using unleavened bread. This phenomenon is not, moreover, a problem confined to liturgy or even the sphere of religion but part of being human – it is easier to follow a groove than to check if it is the best way to do something: 'it is hard to teach an old dog new tricks!' In short, it is relatively easy to produce (but it still might take well over a century) an incarnational theology of the liturgy, but it is relatively difficult to incarnate such an incarnational theology such that it becomes part of our felt memory and experience. Moreover, we like the familiar and we tend to equate 'tradition' with what we saw in our childhood: so in creating a new practice we run counter to a conservative instinct in our nature as ritual animals that makes deep reform (no matter how bizarre our past may be) difficult and unsettling.

So, given that not every action will reflect the formal understanding found in our theology of the liturgy, does the new translation reflect that theology of the incarnation?

An incarnational model of language

One of the constant distractions facing Jesus's followers has been attempts to play down that he was a real human individual: truly a man. He was not

---

[1] See O'Loughlin (2009).

a divinity who appeared as human to provide a user-friendly interface, nor one that absorbed a bit of humanity to give him a taste of being human. Jesus was one with us 'in all but sin', and in his humanity we encounter the fundamental sacrament. So where did our high priest operate: he was not of a priestly family (though Christians since the second century have tried to give him such a background),[2] nor did try to create an alternative to the temple liturgy (as those at Qumran tried to do), but rather he proclaimed a liturgy in the heart of the everyday: in one's room, around the table, in the household, in the fields and in simply prayers where all could address the Father offering both thanks and intercession. And we see this incarnational style being made routine in the early communities.[3]

Just as he restored the creation in himself and whose priesthood was recalled in that the veil of the temple was torn asunder, so his followers recognized that their liturgy was to take place in the midst of their lives. At their tables they were to offer the thanksgiving sacrifice and feast, there in their welcome that broke the most rigid of human boundaries separating people they were to model the heavenly kingdom.[4] Here was the greatest break with the law's model of liturgy: in Leviticus and Numbers the liturgy is characterized by separation, the holy from the unholy, and there is the constant problem of ensuring that impurity does not pollute the things of God. Now, the Lord himself was coming to a human table and with his fellow humans was making the offering of thanks and praise. To engage in the liturgy of the incarnate Lord is to recognize that every aspect of life is holy, and that it is from the heart of the totality of life that we, as the new people, praise God. Impurity now would be the result of the failure to build the kingdom, while the holiness fitting to the Lord's house would be seen in feeding the hungry, clothing the poor, welcoming the outcast and offering reconciliation. This is the significance of the Second Vatican Council's cry that the Eucharist is at the centre of Christian life. This incarnational vision

---

[2] See the Protevangelium of James: Jesus belongs, as does his mother, inside the Jerusalem temple.
[3] See O'Loughlin (2010), 85–104.
[4] See Bradshaw and Johnson (2012), 1–59.

meant that Christianity – alone among the new religions sweeping through the Roman Empire – did not develop an elaborate esoteric cult nor did it require an elaborate ceremonial apparatus – a fact that struck Pliny the Younger, c. 113, when he said that the gathering was simply a meal with some hymns. The sacrality of the Christian gathering was not in a special other-worldly language, their liturgy took place at a table with ordinary food and ordinary language, and the sacrality was based in the understanding that all creation had been made holy though the incarnation.

If this view of Christian liturgy is accepted – and it was a view that had almost no adherents for centuries, when liturgy was imagined using an Old Testament typology – then the notion that there is a special style for liturgy that stresses its *otherness* is highly flawed. Indeed, such a defence of the otherness of liturgical action, vesture, architecture and language, while it may be in accord with a human religious sentiment as expressed in Rudolf Otto's *ganz Andere*, may be adrift of recognizing the radical 'newness' of the Christ. If God is encountered in Jesus in the everyday, then in the everyday events we have the basic liturgy and our encounter with the Father. We, in reflecting on Jesus, do not see a hieratic figure functioning within the then recognized parameters of religious cult, but one who gathers people in their everyday experience and enables them to encounter, there: perhaps around the sinner Zacchaeus's dinner table, the Father's transforming love. But living up to this down the centuries has been a struggle; slipping into the well-worn clichés of 'religious' behaviour has always tended to dull our vision.

A sacred vocabulary

In Mark's account of the Jerusalem Passover meal – which is the paradigm form for the meal being eaten weekly in the churches – we are told that Jesus 'taking a cup (*potērion*) gave thanks' (14.23). *Potērion* is not a sacral word, it is a word from everyday drinking. It has as many of sacral overtones as our word 'mug', but that does not mean that it does not have special significance within the remembered teaching of Jesus. 'For truly I tell you, whoever gives you a cup (*potērion*) of water to drink because you bear the name of Christ will by no means lose the reward' (Mark 9.41); while it is also the image of sharing in the destiny of the Christ through discipleship: 'Are you able to drink the cup (*potērion*) that I drink?' (Mark 10.38 and 39), and it is the symbol of his own loving obedience to the Father: 'Abba, Father, for you all things are possible; remove this cup (*potērion*) from me; yet, not what I want, but what you want.' (Mark 14.36). This exact usage is found in all the parallel Gospel passages and followed the usage already attested in Paul. It was the language of the everyday table that formed the language of the eucharistic table and prompted a key metaphor range of Christians. This is a case of language being a reflection of incarnation.

By the time the Gospels are rendered into Latin this word is translated by the word *calix* – itself borrowed from Greek *kulix* but not found in the Gospels – which does not belong to the messiness of the ordinary. A *calix* is a more elaborate drinking vessel, akin to our word 'goblet', which belongs to the formal toasting at banquets – it is word intended to distinguish its user from the world of the street and set him socially and culturally apart. So the use of *calix*, not *poculus*, in Latin[5] is not an ideal rendering of the Greek but a witness to the constant temptation extrinsically to sacralize the Christ-event by stressing its otherness, its preciousness and so the liturgy's, distance from an everyday table. Now it is possible that this is simply a case that the Latin translations used a more refined register, but this does not dismiss the point that the average family did not think they used *calices* at breakfast: '*calix*' survives in Latin and the vernaculars, solely as a technical ecclesiastical usage.

So, should we render *potērion* as 'cup' – a word in our normal discourse as in 'do you want a cup of coffee' or 'I will get you a cup of water' or a word that only belongs to a special ritual vocabulary? Clearly, it is these precise ritual tones that have made it attractive to the new translators, it echoes a Latin steeped in formal ritual and elegance, not the world of tea, coffee, kettles and sinks. And in so far as it leans towards that sacral otherness and

---

[5] Our word 'cup' is derived from cuppa, but when cuppa came into use in Latin (it comes from cupa = 'a cask') is uncertain; early uses of cuppa suggest we translate it as 'tankard'.

away from the ordinary, it is inadequate to reflect the original Gospel texts it seeks to echo and a symptom of a less than thorough-going grasp of an incarnational liturgy.

'Barbecue' Language

We are told that the new translation's language more accurately reflects the Latin, and that it is a more worthy language for liturgy's serious nature. If we leave aside what constitutes an accurate reflection of one language in another as a matter of linguistic theory, the second claim comes heavy laden with theological presuppositions. There is an implicit claim that only what is distinct from the everyday can be worthy of the service of God. It is the otherness – in whatever form it manifests itself – of the language from that of people communicating with one another, working with one another and seeking to love and care for one another that makes it worthy and appropriate for worship. This view of the nature of the interaction of God and humanity is not confined to supporters of this translation. Many religions have employed cultic languages because these conveyed *the difference* between the human world and that of the gods. The use of hieroglyphs on the Rosetta stone, of Sanskrit in Indian religious texts, of Old Church Slavonic, classical Armenian and Latin in Christianity are all instances of this phenomenon.[6] In every case these special languages are archaic forms whose place as 'sacred' status is due to ritual continuing to use a language that had been abandoned in everyday use by the majority and had become the preserve of the ritual specialists; but even if it is a widespread religious phenomenon, that does not mean that it accords well with our Christian confession that the Lord is with us *today*.

This problem with the new translation was brought home to me in a rather paradoxical way when I heard that an Australian bishop had expressed his negative judgement of the previous translation by characterizing it as 'barbecue language'. It is worth studying this expression: the bishop wanted to communicate succinctly, effectively, memorably, and in a way by which everyone would understand and appreciate not just his words, but

---

[6] See O'Loughlin (2012)

his message. So what did he do? He used everyday language, a metaphor from the ordinary lives of Australians and a word that graphically carries its message. Why did he not wish the precision of calling it 'quotidian language' (using a Latin root) or 'profane language' (echoing the theory of religious language in which he appears to operate)? When it was important to get a message across, he chose the ordinary quotidian term 'barbecue' – which suggests that he must appreciate in some inchoate way that many of the expressions of the translation, which he consciously praises, will simply not communicate!

Now let us think, positively, about that designation of the 1973 texts as 'barbecue language'. The barbecue is an informal gathering of friends whose very informality stresses the equality of those present (one could not have a 'high table' at a 'barbi'), it belongs to everyday life (at least in certain climates), it expresses joyful relaxation, and it can easily welcome additional people in a way that other kinds of eating cannot. Moreover, it is at such gatherings that community is built up, friends meet, and we become, celebrate and rejoice over who we are. In many ways, the barbecue fulfils many of the functions that were performed by the eucharistic meals of the early churches – and dropped out, as the Eucharist became the name of a specific sacral ritual. It is not accidental that many churches and communities today organize barbecues and 'pot luck suppers' precisely to build up a sense of community, offering members an opportunity to meet and to affirm the ecclesial nature of discipleship. Far from being an insult to the 1973 translation, as that bishop intended, the designation 'barbecue language' (or its analogues in more rain-sodden churches) might be seen as a desired standard for liturgical language – provided that one has a robust theology of incarnation at the heart of one's view of liturgy. By contrast, a theory of religious language that conforms to a widespread religious instinct (going far beyond Christianity's bounds) may be wholly inappropriate to the pattern of divine revelation we confess when we say that ours is an incarnational religion.

Task

The new translation is with us – and many simply say that we must 'get over it, get used to it' (and it is a fact that, once one puts up with something, eventually perceptions of inadequacy fade). However, in the longer term the problems will mount. The rite as promulgated in 1969 removed the glaring inadequacies of a previous rite, sought to curtail its grosser practices and to provide a liturgy which could be used by the whole people in a way that coheres with our ecclesiology.[7] But it was still far from being the genuinely community event that can lie at the heart of a community. This is the real task we should now be tackling. The new translation is filled with a curious nostalgia for a liturgy that belonged to the individual priest and a priest's private spirituality, as was made possible by the uniformity of printing and a written language foreign all who used it. This may be seen as a regrettable stalling, but conversely may force the more radical questions about the future of our worship, inherent in the Council's reforms, to the fore.[8] And if that liturgy is not incarnational in its intrinsic logic, its grounding in human nature, and in the world it creates, it will be unworthy.

---

[7] See J. Dallen, 'What kind of ecclesiology?' at misguidemissal.com (accessed 22 June 2012).
[8] See O'Loughlin (2012).

5

Where are the Voices of Women in the Roman Liturgy?

Patricia Rumsey

One of the objections to the new translation of the Roman Missal is its inconsistent use of inclusive language. Although the new translation of the *Gloria* gives us hope in its rendering of 'all people of good will', this hope is dashed when we come to the infamous 'For us men and for our salvation' in the new text of the Creed. This inconsistency continues in the various Prefaces. Women wonder if they are included at all in Christ's work of salvation, when Common Preface II is used: 'For in your goodness you created man and, when he was justly condemned, in mercy you redeemed him ...'.

But as the apogee of insensitivity we might quote Eucharistic Prayer IV:

> You formed man in your own image
> and entrusted the whole world to his care,
> so that in serving you alone, the Creator,
> he might have dominion over all creatures.
>
> And when through disobedience he had lost
> your friendship, you did not abandon him to
> the domain of death.

By this inconsistent use of language, women – and therefore two-thirds of most worshipping congregations – are all but excluded, and their voices are not heard. In our secular society today much importance is given to the metaphor of 'voice': it is recognized that each group in society has a right to be heard. However, in the history of the Church, God's revelation and our response in liturgical prayer has been almost exclusively mediated in male voices. The voices of women have been all but silent. In 1987, the late Pia Buxton said that our church is 'fundamentally lop-sided' in 'its stance, voice and authority system', because it is 'male, celibate and clerical in its decision-making'. I agree with her that 'there is a place for celibacy and a need for the clerical', and I also agree 'that men are wonderful', but this overwhelmingly male control-system means that the Church is anachronistic and lacking in credibility in today's world. It must make women more visible in ministry, liturgy and authority.

I will focus here on this absence of women in the liturgy and the vocabulary and the theology of liturgical prayer. The issue of inclusive language in the new translation is being given much attention, but we need to look deeper and examine what our use of language reveals about our perception of holiness and how this relates to issues of gender. The liturgical year as we now celebrate it according to the Universal Calendar all but silences the voices of women. For example, very few of the second readings used during the Office of Readings in the Roman Breviary are taken from the works of women writers, and, when women are mentioned specifically, they are usually presented as weak and ineffectual. In the actual number of saints whose offices are celebrated in the course of the liturgical year, male saints far outnumber female saints; there are 146 men saints in comparison with 30 women saints.

However, if we believe that the divine image includes both masculine and feminine (Gen.1.26), then to exclude the feminine means that our image of God has become sadly inadequate. The Talmud understood that the image of God in the human race is only complete when man and woman are joined together in the married state. So thus to emphasize the masculine at the expense of the feminine, means that half the human race has been excluded from humanity's interaction with the divine and our vision of God has been diminished. The result has been an inadequate representation of women within the Church and an inadequate appreciation of the feminine contribution to the Church. Building on the principle of *lex orandi; lex credendi* and assuming that the form and content of our prayer is indicative of our underlying belief structures, this paper examines the way in which the voices of women have been ignored in Christian history and thus have not been accorded a rightful place in the liturgy. This neglect continues today in the new translation of the Roman Missal; the voices of women are strangely absent.

Throughout the Christian centuries, the Church has always accorded the highest honour to the Mother of Jesus and by upholding belief in her perpetual virginity has set out for the emulation of the faithful one of the archetypal ideals of the feminine. On the other hand, by upholding the example of repentant sinners such as Mary Magdalene,[1] the Church encourages the ideal of penitence. A cursory glance at the overall spectrum of hagiography in the Roman Church might see it as all-encompassing, but a closer perusal reveals that it is so restricted in its understanding of female holiness that it cannot present a woman saint independently of her sexual status; women saints are invariably listed according to their relations or lack of relations with men. So there is no place in the way Catholicism celebrates its self-perception in its cycles of liturgical prayer for a single woman who is neither a virgin nor a harlot. This is a damning condemnation of the understanding of feminine holiness and the way it is set forth in Western worship, and yet a trawl through the Common Offices of Saints reveals that in the stakes for sanctity men can be 'apostles', or 'martyrs', or 'pastors', or 'doctors' or just plain 'holy men', whereas women have only the options

---

[1] The remembered image of Mary Magdalene is, however, a composite of several women found in the gospel narratives: Mark 16.9 merely says that Jesus had cast out from her seven demons – so she was a 'demoniac' not a 'sinner' – and this image of her in Mark is taken up by Luke 8.2 where she is named as one of those women who went with Jesus and 'The Twelve' on their travels. The notion that she was a 'sinner' is a conflation of Mary Magdalene with an un-named woman in Luke 7.37–9; the combination is then conflated with the 'Mary' mentioned in John 11.2 and 12.3. This composite of the fallen, repentant woman ignores the fact that the principal role of Mary Magdalene in the Synoptic Tradition is as a witness to the death and burial of Jesus – she is one of those few who were followers until the end (a theme also found in John 19.25) – as in Mark 15.40, 47 and 16.1 (and parallels); while in Matthew (28.1) and Luke (24.10) she is presented as a primary witness to the resurrection.

of 'virgins' or 'holy women' – with a sidelong glance at 'doctors of the Church'. However, even this picture, grim as it may be, is an improvement on the *Breviarium Romanum* in use prior to Vatican II, where the options for women were unapologetically explicit: *'Commune Unius Virginis'* or *'Commune Unius Non Virginis'*. Male saints have never been thus categorized according to their sexual experience or lack of it. So if the liturgical year as we now celebrate it all but silences the voices of Christian women, especially those who were married (and their absence creates a very big silence indeed), what do we need to do to redress this balance?

Our first task in constructing a more genuinely representative sanctoral cycle, which will help to give women their rightful voice in the Church is to develop a new model of female sanctity, which acknowledges that alongside virgins and widows, married women who are living an active sexual life can be authentically holy. At present, in the cycles of liturgical worship, they are very much 'second class citizens'. The traditional theology of sanctity as it was understood until Vatican II has been based on a negative world-view: holiness, especially for women, was only seen as possible of attainment by rejecting 'the world', fleeing from it – either by martyrdom (in the early centuries) or by a life of seclusion and asceticism in 'the desert' (from the fourth century onwards), or in the convent and by setting up physical barriers to keep 'the world' at bay. However, Vatican II brought with it a positive and world-affirming theology which emphasized the goodness of the world and showed the possibility for all people of finding their way to holiness within this world, not outside it. This realization has been described as 'foundation-shaking'. By this issue of rethinking the possibility of attaining holiness, the Council had reversed the centuries-long 'adversary stance' of the Church in relation to the world. No longer was the religious life seen as the only 'call to perfection'; the Council now proposed a 'universal call to holiness' for all the faithful.

Apparently the Church authorities had done a *volte-face* – now, in sharp contradistinction to the earlier stance, Vatican II expressed a view which saw 'the world' as good, even holy. No longer were religious the only ones pledged to a life of 'evangelical perfection'. Now the Council's Dogmatic Constitution on the Church (*Lumen gentium*) revealed that the laity were being called to holiness, too! This epoch-making pronouncement of the Council was truly ground-breaking in that it brought back into sharp focus the awareness of the holiness of the whole living community that we find in the letters of Paul. Here it is emphasized that through baptism human persons are put right with God in Christ and become sharers in the divine nature. Lest anyone doubt the result, the council says it plainly: 'In this way they are made holy' (n. 40). In this decree, Vatican II reversed the centuries-old negative world view according to which the whole material world had to be kept at arm's length. The human body especially was seen as a source of sin, and it has been this dualistic world-view, which has seen all created matter as – at best, a distraction; at worst, as evil – which has seen women as the source of all temptation and therefore an evil to be shunned. Now, we begin to see creation – and maybe even women – in a positive light.

So with this explicit understanding of the holiness of all creation, Vatican II has returned to a model of sanctity propounded by Paul, when he wrote letters 'To all God's beloved in Rome who are called to be saints' (Rom. 1.1). Paul's personal greeting at the end of his letter to the Romans includes several women. We have no way of knowing whether these women were married, but we can assume that those named in conjunction with a man were married to him. Thus Prisca and Aquila, Andronicus and Junia and the mother of Rufus were all commended by Paul and held up as examples of faith and ministry to other Christians. But we do not commemorate these women liturgically, and Junia, 'prominent among the apostles' got airbrushed out of Paul's letters very early on. She thus became one of the many women who disappeared from view and lost their rightful places in the written records of the Church. One wonders how many other exceptional women have vanished without trace from the pages of Christian hagiography, because their lives were not thought worthy of recording.

The ongoing problem with women in the Church is that they have consistently been seen as a temptation to male virtue. This was noticed by a young woman visiting Rome in the late nineteenth century:

> I still can't understand why it's so easy for a woman to get
> excommunicated in Italy! All the time people seemed to

be saying: 'No, you mustn't go here, you mustn't go there; you'll be excommunicated.' There's no respect for us poor wretched women anywhere ...

The young woman expressing herself so forcefully was Thérèse Martin, the future St. Thérèse of Lisieux; she too experienced in her own day the misogynist attitude of clerics in the Church and made her feelings known. We could perhaps point out in passing that her parents have been beatified, and yet their marriage was far from 'normal', in that they lived as brother and sister for the first nine months of their life together and only began to live a regular married life after the intervention of Madame Martin's confessor. This attitude to sexuality typifies the way sanctity was interpreted at that time; to be holy one had to be asexual

Throughout the Christian centuries nearly all theologians have been men, also all confessors, spiritual writers and directors. The result of this overwhelmingly masculine influence on the spiritual lives of women has been to inculcate a masculine approach to and way of living out the life of the Spirit that has all but negated the experience of the women themselves. The result has been for male spiritual guides to inculcate in women the need to avoid specifically male failings such as aggressiveness, pride, homosexuality, disregard for hierarchical authority and similar vices. But they have not helped women to identify the failings to which their own natures make them more prone: pettiness, lack of self-esteem, envy, manipulation, fear and timidity.

That this attitude of male, and especially clerical, superiority was still alive and well in the late twentieth century can be seen from the following passage in which the author was instructing the clergy in their preaching duties:

One must use simple language for the women. Substantives and those difficult compound words which commonly encumber our language should be avoided as much as possible. Technical terms and foreign words must be explained if they cannot be avoided. They are indispensable and self-explanatory for the priest, who is steeped in the classics, but women often do not understand them at all or only imperfectly. They are patient listeners but they are easily intimidated by bombastic expressions. It is unfortunate that women can hardly read the papal encyclicals or learn from them on account of their classical style, or perhaps more so on account of the defective and clumsy translations.

Though published originally in Germany in 1958, this book was translated into English and published in 1964, thus providing evidence that such misogyny was still to be encountered in Catholic writing in comparatively recent times; almost unbelievably, it was written by a woman.

These attitudes are detrimental to the Church's theology, both in theory and in practical expression and insulting to women themselves. They need to become truly a thing of the past, and women, both married and religious, need to be given their rightful place as examples of holy Christian living and intercession in the cycle of the liturgy. A first step, and one that would be far easier than setting out a whole new calendar, would be the consistent use of inclusive language in the missal and encouragement from the hierarchy that such language be employed with corresponding sensitivity everywhere in the liturgy, as they have ordered that the new translation be used *ad litteram*. This would ensure that the voices of women were not being silenced, and their presence in the worshipping congregation was being acknowledged.

6

'Pro multis': 'for you and for ...' who?

Janet E. Rutherford

At the heart of the eucharistic liturgy lie liturgical words that we are invited to interiorize as our own most intimate conversation with God. Our attention might stray at times during Mass, but we all instinctively attend to the Eucharistic Prayer, and particularly the Words of Institution. Any change to those words therefore affects us at our most spiritually vulnerable moment, and it is therefore a matter of urgency to reflect upon the fact that Christ's blood is now not to be said to have been shed 'for you and for all', but 'for you and for many'. It is impossible for the thought not to pop into our heads, 'Did Christ not die for all mankind?' This introduces a doubt about the most fundamental Christian belief and is a potential source of confusion.

It should first be noted that Benedict XVI has made it clear that he was aware of this; but he believes that there is something important at stake in the use of the words 'for many'. As he stated in his *Letter to the German Bishops*:

> The question immediately arises: if Jesus died for all, then
> why did he say 'for many' at the Last Supper?

Before exploring answers to this, we need to be clear about what we can know about what Christ 'said'. For one thing, he was speaking in Aramaic; but his words were recorded in Greek. And in addition, the New Testament gives four accounts of the words Christ used during the Last Supper, none of which is identical with another. The oldest, in 1 Corinthians 11.24f reads:

> This is my body which is **for you**. Do this in remembrance of me. … This cup is the new covenant in my blood. Do this as often as **you** drink it, in remembrance of me.

The next oldest is Mark 14.22ff:

> **Take**; this is my body'. And he took a cup … and **they all drank** from it. And he said to them, 'This is my blood of the new covenant, which is poured out **for many**.

Of the two other synoptic Gospels, Luke is closer to Paul, and Matthew to Luke. Thus:

> This is my body which is given **for you**. Do this in remembrance of me … This cup which is poured out **for you** is the new covenant in my blood. (Luke 22.19f)

> '**Take**, eat, this is my body'. And he took a cup … saying, '**Drink** of it, all of **you**; for this is my blood of the covenant, which is poured out **for many** for the forgiveness of sins.' (Matt. 26.26ff)

Thus, all four agree that the bread is Christ's body given 'for you' – that is, for the disciples gathered with him at the time. Mark and Matthew make this clear by the words 'Take' – a command to those present. In the same way, all four make it clear that the cup is 'for you' – that is, for those present. Although only Luke says 'for you', Paul, Mark and Matthew all command those present ('you') to drink. The current problem arises from the fact that Mark and Matthew add, together with those present, a reference to Christ's blood being shed for 'many'.

What does this mean? Everyone is agreed that in the whole rite, whatever the exact words Christ used, he was identifying himself with the Suffering Servant of Isaiah. Matthew in particular was always on the lookout for ways to identify Jesus with Old Testament prophecy. In the twentieth century, liturgical scholars were able to benefit from advances in biblical scholarship, which had done much to elucidate the meaning of the Hebrew used in the context of the Suffering Servant (which was translated into Greek and then into Latin as 'many'). It is the Hebrew that will have been in Christ's thoughts as he spoke in Aramaic. Scholarly opinion today on the original meaning of the 'many' remains just as it was half a century ago, when Joachim Jeremias wrote:

> [In] the pre-Christian interpretations of the 'many' in Isaiah 53 … it is certain that by 'the many' the Gentiles are meant. The Wisdom of Solomon … interprets the 'many' (Isaiah 52.14–15) as the sinners who have afflicted the righteous … and had him in derision … and since [there is] no distinction between Jews and Gentiles in this passage, it is probable that it refers to the godless among Jews and Gentiles alike, but in the first instance … to the latter. These pre-Christian interpretations are of special weight because of their agreement with the meaning of the original text. … For he saw himself as the servant of whom it is said in Isaiah 49.6, that he should not only 'restore the preserved of Israel' but be given 'also for a light to the Gentiles that you may be my salvation unto the end of the earth'. Therefore *peri pollōn* [for many] in the words of institution has not … an exclusive meaning (many, but not all) but … an inclusive meaning (the sum total, consisting of many). Accordingly the translation of *to peri pollōn ekchunnomenon* has to be: 'which is going to be shed for the whole world'.

It has thus come as a great surprise to biblical scholars to read in Benedict XVI's *Letter to the German Bishops* that the scholarly exegetical consensus about this 'has collapsed … it no longer exists'. There has in fact been no 'collapse' of scholarly agreement; so the statement that consensus 'no longer exists' can only mean that the consensus that *does* exist is no longer accepted by the 'magisterium'. Why is this?

When Benedict XVI asks whether, by translating 'many' as 'all',

> the question is raised as to whether the text of the Bible is
> not being misrepresented, whether perhaps an element of
> untruth has been brought into the most sacred place in our
> worship?

The answer of biblical scholarship, following Jeremias, is 'No'. If on the other hand we ask ourselves, is there something in the original meaning of 'many' that we lose by saying 'all', the answer is: yes – but it is a matter of emphasis. The Aramaic that Jesus would have spoken, echoing the Hebrew of Isaiah, would have meant more than just 'all' – it will have meant 'for absolutely everyone, especially those who are about to kill me!' This exegesis gives a wonderful deepening to our understanding of Christ's complete and unconditionally loving offering of himself. But this is not conveyed by the words 'for many'. 'For many' suggests that there are limits to those for whom Christ died; which is, as we have seen, precisely the opposite to the meaning of the underlying Hebrew and Aramaic. How are we then to be faithful to the Greek words recorded in the New Testament, while at the same time conveying the sense of the Hebrew and Aramaic that underlie them?

First of all we must understand that *all* Christian liturgies conflate the four New Testament accounts of the words of institution, in different ways. The question is how best to do so to convey what Christ meant by comparing himself to the Suffering Servant. The liturgies of St Chrysostom, St Basil, St Mark and the Anglican *Book of Common Prayer* all combine the words over the cup as 'for you and for many'. The *Book of Common Prayer*, however, gives an 'exegesis' of this in the words of administration: 'The body of our Lord Jesus Christ, which was given for thee …', 'The blood of our Lord Jesus Christ, which was shed for thee …' This is intended to reinforce the point that, just as Christ offered himself to the disciples gathered around him at the Last Supper, he offers himself to those 'many' who come to receive him in the Eucharist.

In *God Is Near Us: The Eucharist, the Heart of Life*, Benedict XVI makes it clear that it is precisely this point that he wishes to convey in the use of 'many'. At (it must be said) bewildering length, it becomes evident that what he is asserting is (to paraphrase) this: 'It is clear from biblical evidence and tradition that Christ died for all mankind. But since humanity has free will, not everyone will receive him. Thus the "you" in the words of institution referred, at the Last Supper, to the disciples gathered with him; and they refer in our Eucharist to the faithful gathered to receive him.' But this is not what comes to our minds when we hear 'for many'. It is arguable that of all the liturgical conflations of the New Testament words, that of Luther best achieves what Ratzinger is aiming at. As we have seen, 'you' is implicit in all the accounts. Lutherans therefore only use the word 'you'. They do this precisely in order to make the point that the grace conveyed by the Sacrament is only efficacious to those who receive it. Thus, Luther (who knew his New Testament inside out) has in his 'Small Catechism':

> Our Lord Jesus Christ, on the night when he was betrayed, took the bread, and when he had given thanks, he broke it and gave it to his disciples and said, Take; eat; this is my body which is given for you. Do this in remembrance of me. In the same way he also took the cup after the supper, and when he had given thanks, he gave it to them saying, Drink of it, all of you. This cup is the New Testament in my blood, shed for you for the forgiveness of sins. Do this, as often as you drink it, in remembrance of me.

It is therefore indeed not necessary to re-introduce 'many' to achieve what Benedict XVI is trying to accomplish. No one in the Roman Church believes that everyone will be saved just because Christ died for everyone (especially since it is becoming increasingly clear what a dire fate awaits those who disagree with the 'magisterium'!) The use of the translation 'for all' has not resulted in a pandemic of universalism. If anything, it reinforces Ratzinger's own understanding of Christ's sacrifice being effective for those who receive him. If the translation instruction *Liturgiam authenticam* makes it necessary to use 'many' or nothing, it is surely preferable to have nothing: just exclude the word and stick with 'for you' (who come forward to receive). The consensus (which *does* exist) about the meaning of 'many' in Isaiah identifies the 'many' with sinners who betray Christ – that is, precisely, with 'us' – the 'you' to whom Christ offers himself when we come to receive him.

What is certain is that, given that universalism is not rampant in the Roman Church, 'all' was not doing any harm. To insert 'many', however, runs the very real risk of inviting the opposite heresy: predestination. Saying that Christ died 'for many' has in fact always been a proof text of Predestinarians in the West. The Epistle to the Romans in particular is full of references to 'the elect', and with the publication in the fifteenth century of the complete works of Augustine, the entire Latin-speaking world had access to his most extreme interpretation of Romans in his attacks on Pelagius. Thus, in the sixteenth and seventeenth centuries, Predestinationism very nearly overwhelmed all of western Christianity and continues to divide those ecclesial communities that are commonly lumped together as 'protestant'. It is therefore disconcerting to see how little this threat seems to worry Benedict XVI. He writes lightly of the Jansenist virus:

> [I]n the seventeenth century there was an explicit condemnation of a Jansenist proposition that asserted that Christ did not die for everyone. This limitation of salvation was thus explicitly rejected as an erroneous teaching that contradicted the faith of the whole Church.

It is as if, because Predestinationism was condemned by the Church in the seventeenth century, it is incapable of becoming, once again, the pernicious infection that it was then. But that virus is alive in Western Christianity today; and stating that Christ died 'for many' opens the door and invites it back in.

To counter this possibility, the German bishops have been asked to do a very strange thing. They have been told to introduce words that the Pope himself knows will cause confusion; and they are then to counter this confusion by undertaking a special work of catechesis for clergy, which clergy will replicate for the laity. This catechesis will explain to everyone that 'many' means 'all', but that not all will accept Christ. But everyone knows that already. If the translation instruction *Liturgiam authenticam* makes it impossible to translate 'many' as 'all', then simply leave it out. There is no ambiguity in 'you'.

There is indeed a great potential source of danger in tinkering with the wording of the words of institution in order to make complex theological points. To write about theology, even to teach it to parish groups, is one thing. There is time to tease out the inner significance of biblical texts. But as we approach the altar of God we ought to turn off our dialectical faculties together with our mobile phones and just listen to the still, small voice of God. There simply isn't time during the act of communion to sort out what might be meant by 'the many'. There is in any case no guarantee that people would turn up for the catechetical classes, or that if they did they would understand the arguments, or that if they did both they would remember the theological exegesis when hearing the words of the liturgy. To undertake a catechetical project that would demand so much time and organization, and the success of which is questionable, could only be justified if there were an extremely vital dogmatic truth under threat; something that affects our understanding of the very foundations of the Christian faith – the nature of the Person of Christ, for example, or the means of our salvation. If there isn't, then the devotional life of the people that is rooted in the Eucharist should be treated with reverence and not as a theological exercise. They should be allowed to receive the sacrament in trust, so that God's offering of himself may enter their hearts unhindered. This is emphatically not the place to sow seeds of doubt.

7

Traduttore – traditore?
The New Translation and Mission

John Ball

And here's to dear old Boston,
the land of the bean and the cod,
where the Lowells talk to the Cabots
and the Cabots talk only to God.
(Toast at Harvard dinner, 1919)

In the course of the 1974 Roman Bishops' Synod on Evangelization in the Modern World (out of which arose Pope Paul VI's *Evangelii nuntiandi*) the African bishops issued a statement rejecting as completely out-of-date 'the so-called theology of adaptation'. What is the significance of this for the act of translating? I believe it has significance not just in 'the mission fields' but everywhere.

The cross-cultural missionary coming to a socio-culture different from his own, speaking a language different to his /her own is immediately faced with the problem of translation, not simply from one language into another, but from one pattern of socio-cultural perception to another. When the apostles first proclaimed, they did so in their own society, and Paul, when he began to travel, went first to the synagogues of the *diaspora*. It was only as the word travelled further abroad that issues of language and culture arose. For instance, in 597, Augustine was sent from his monastery in Rome by Pope Gregory to convert the English. As he crossed France, Augustine wrote back complaining that the Christianity he was encountering was not identical to what he knew in Rome. Gregory replied saying that of course it differed – he was not in Rome – and when he reached the Angles he should not impose Roman ways. When he reached England, Augustine did not encounter any language problem, for the court communicated in Latin with him. But, in spite of this common medium, the Irish missionaries in the North of England were introducing practices that differed in some areas from Augustine's, though these were not theologically significant. It was later, as the gospel spread to the 'barbarian' pagan tribes of Europe that more problems arose. When Luther began to question Roman centralization, the reaction was for Trent to attempt to impose one, universally identical pattern – a standard practice, of liturgy, sacrament and theology. Go into any Catholic church, anywhere in the world and the same Latin Mass would be found being repeated – that was the theory, at least.

The African bishops' complaint was that, up to the nineteenth century, this proclamation had not encountered sub-Saharan Africa. When it did, the proclamation was not just of sacrament and theology, but sacrament and theology proclaimed via a European understanding that was imposed – the missionaries were merely 'adapting'. The number of West African Christians baptized 'Patrick' is significant pointer to the deeper mindset. The Holy Week services in Seville and Manila bear great similarity. West African and Filipino Christianities betray the national identities of the original evangelists! This may have been less true in India where there was a strong social culture that pre-dated that of Europe, with its own strong philosophical and religious traditions.

From 1583 to 1600, the Italian missionary Matteo Ricci worked in China. It is significant that he was Italian, for in the fifteenth century the Pope had drawn a line down the middle of the Atlantic and declared lands to the East of the line to be under Portuguese patronage, whilst those to the West were under Spain. Hence the missionaries in China were, for the most part Portuguese Franciscans. Ricci, pushed by his superior, Valignano, learned Mandarin and studied Confucianism, attempting to re-state Christianity in terms of Confucian philosophy. When there was complaint that Confucianism was pagan, Ricci countered that this was not significant as it was a philosophy not a theology. Aquinas had encountered the same objection when he began to re-write theology in terms of Aristotle rather than the Platonism of Augustine. Such attempts go far beyond adaptation.

Adaptation is essentially dualistic. As nominalism does with language, it assumes there is an essential fixed, carved-in-stone, essence which can be transported worldwide and adapted to any new territory. A parallel is when you transport your hair-dryer, fit an adaptor to match the local current, and the machine works equally well everywhere and performs exactly the same operation in every location. The philosophical teaching of nominalism consists in holding 'that general terms have no corresponding reality either in or out of the mind, being merely words'. A rose is a rose is a rose and smells as sweet, however it is named. Whether you pray kneeling or in the lotus position, whether you wear black or unbleached cloth for mourning, whether you play an organ or strike drums is irrelevant, it is the same hidden spiritual effect that is being achieved. It is, after all, God who works the effect, so he (or she!) could cleanse from sin at the pouring of water or anointing with oil, or massaging with goose-fat or tincture of arnica – there is no particular need for baptism to be exclusively by the pouring of water, God is not constrained by our limitations. This is sacramental nominalism and ignores the incarnation and the incarnate nature of sacraments. Nominalism ignores the fact that God works in and through our bodies – there is nothing in the mind or soul that has not come through our senses – and so God is constrained by his creation. To hold other would make God irrational. So baptism, to be baptism and to achieve what it does, must use the pouring of water – a rose by another name is something else.

The Manchester school of anthropology, from the immensely influential Bronislaw Malinowski (1884–1942) onwards, was dedicated to the notion of 'functionalism'. Malinowski held that anthropology is a science, and science is empirical, so all anthropological recording must be confined to *sensibilia*, to what can be recorded with camera and tape-recorder. This limits the record to behavioural and representational patternings. All cultural processes are treated as reified objects and the underlying structuring of cultural behaviour is discounted. Any attempt to identify this would be non-scientific. But to remain at this level is to miss the culture's making of meaning where the native's competence will always exceed that of the observer. John Searle explored this approach by imaging a room called 'the Chinese Room'. On one side messages are handed in to be translated. The person in the room doesn't know any Chinese, but has a list of characters and instructions, so that, blindly following the instructions, he eventually hands out a 'translation' in Chinese on the other side of the room. For Searle, this is not translation, for it ignores meaning: it is just the act of substituting empty signs – but these do not in themselves constitute language. The human being is essentially a maker of meaning.

And there is something else at fault here. For, if we remain at the behavioural and representational level, ignoring the underlying meaning-making, then we will note the empirical behaviour of the other, record it and interpret it in terms of our own cultural meaning-making. We will interpret in terms of Western philosophical and scientific constructs what may well be non-scientific and of another philosophical background. We will interpret functionalistically, what is essentially semantic. We will record a rain dance and conclude the dancer is trying to cause rain to fall. This is confounding different categories of discourse.

Nominalism operates in the same way with words. The nominalist sees words as arbitrary signs having no intrinsic attachment to their reference. This word here indicates that thing over there. But this confuses sign with symbol; whereas, in reality, they are different. All signs operate, for nominalists, in the manner of road signs: a steel pole with a triangle of metal on top of it bearing a picture of a girl and boy conventionally tells us there is a school further along. For the nominalist who sees words as merely signs, *canis* = dog = *ido* (the Hiligaynon word). It makes no difference which you use; all three refer you to that thing over there wagging its tail. Likewise, *vir* = man = *tao*. But words are not signs but symbols: each one brings an aura of socio-cultural associations with it. An '*ido*' can be eaten, we don't eat our dogs. '*Tao*' is gender-free, it means a person, and you have to ask, is the person male or female?

And it is not just a matter of whether or not we eat dogs. In English, a female dog is a bitch, the perfectly correct word, but, unless you are a dog-breeder, it is not a word used without any feeling for its associations. We speak of 'a dog's life', a 'dirty dog', a 'gay dog' (maybe a bit dated that one), 'dogged', a 'dog-leg', a 'bitch', a 'vixen' or a 'cur'. A Kalahari bushman hunts with his dog. He cuddles up with his dog for warmth during the cold desert nights. A very cold night is a 'two-dog night'. The sound or written word is only a surface phenomenon. The words we use are part of our structured social code. Where a native speaker can decipher a distorted sample easily, the non-native user will find difficulty. My English-speaking, Argentinean friend has trouble in Glasgow!

For some time, those interested in the possibility of intelligent life on other planets have transmitted radio signals as mathematical series, one dot, then two dots, then three … or two dots, four dots, six dots … or a group of three, four and five dots, the ratio of the sides of a right-angled triangle. The argument being that any rational society will share in the universal, a-cultural, logical system that is maths, and that they will have deduced Pythagoras's Theorem (as, indeed, the Chinese did before Pythagoras). Prime numbers, it is said, will be found in the outer-most galaxies, however many millennia later. Everybody can communicate in the 'language' of maths. Or there is the parallel case of the language of science, where universally, the letter 'K' means one atom of the element potassium, atomic number 19, free of any associated meaning. The 'languages' of maths and science are artificial, unemotional and cross-cultural. They mean identically the same the world over – do they not?

One might suspect that, in some quarters, there is the notion that Latin within the Roman Catholic Church operates in the same way, free of all cultural association: its meaning is universally identically the same. '*Oremus*' means the same in Reykjavik and Uzbekistan, for Thai Buddhists and Oxford atheists. Only, of course, it doesn't: real languages don't work like maths and science (or as we sometimes, naively, imagine they work). The translator is caught, not just between different words, but between different socio-cultural structurings. When the Spanish missionaries arrived in the Philippines and wanted to speak of 'the Lamb of God', they were faced with a society that had no concept of sheep or lambs since they had never seen or heard any. And the acceptable word for 'God' was debatable, since Filipino society of that day recognized a whole world of spirits, witches and other non-physical beings, good or bad. So the missionaries translated only one word and 'the Lamb of God' is '*Cordero sang Dios*' in the Philippines: the words '*cordero*' and '*Dios*' being left in Spanish.

And if we are to translate a Latin text, we are faced with both synchronic and the diachronic problems, to go from one socio-culture to another and to go from one age to another. In his *Blessed Rage for Order*, the Chicago theologian David Tracy investigates the present pluralism of theologies, from what we might call traditional or fundamentalist to radical where the stress is on the secular. He assumes that every theologian is attempting to interpret the symbols and texts of our common life and of Christianity. How do I, a chaplain in a twenty-first century, Catholic, London, secondary school, proclaim the gospel in such a manner that the pupils will find its relevance to their present-day experience? Tracy points out that such a proclamation must be both adequate to the understanding and acceptance of the listener and at the same time appropriate to the Christian tradition. The theologians, and the translators take their stand along a continual spectrum ranging from the extremely conservative, who may seek simply to re-iterate some early definition, to the radical secularist who ignores the transcendent. The Anglican theologian Don Cupitt gives as his definition of God, and he stresses this is a definition: 'God is the sum of our values'. Such strong secular affirmation Tracy sees as theistic negation. Less far along the line, the liberal theologian is committed to the basic cognitive and ethical claims of our modern secular era. The conservative finds these claims theologically irrelevant. A debate, a couple of years ago, in the General Synod of the Church of England over the ordination of women bishops, illustrates the dilemma. Archbishop Rowan Williams suggested that the Church of England 'appears to be wilfully blind to the changes in society'. *The Times* accused the Church of 'drifting away from common sense', whilst the *Guardian* said 'the process was hi-jacked by a small, highly-motivated group of fundamentalists more interested in strict orthodoxy than in the real world and how people live their lives'. We would not expect *The Times* or the *Guardian* to grasp the theological issues, but they drew attention to problems of translation. The closer I stick to the original language, the further I am from the language into which I am translating. And if I am translating Latin Eucharistic Prayers, the fear of straying from orthodoxy might constrain my efforts at achieving contemporary understanding.

'*Consubstantialem Patri*' is a Latin attempt at Nicaea's attempt to put the infinite mystery of God into finite human language, an attempt that used the then current concepts of Greek philosophy. But if our philosophical understanding of person is different, how will 'consubstantial with the Father' help us? It may be thought that Nicaea and Chalcedon had the last word, but of course, they couldn't have. They are limited attempts to grasp in human language what is beyond language. Philosophies, insights, social structures all change, and theology must attempt continually to re-state the mystery in adequate language. Councils operate under the guidance of the Spirit, but the words are human words. What Denzinger offers us is, at best, 'no entry' signs rather than one-way streets.

The translator then, holds two socio-cultural meaning systems alongside one another. Latin is given to subordinate clauses, English isn't; and to use a multiplicity of clauses in English is simply to cloud the meaning. The use of technical jargon, such as 'prevenient', is an attempt to avoid the multivalency of words; it seeks to avoid our everyday English where words carry a world of associated meanings. It appropriates a thirteenth-century solution to a theological problem of which few will be aware. It is not English. The whole symbolic system of language is an appropriation of the world around us. Whoever first went among the Eskimos must have had trouble with 'The Lord is my Shepherd.' And indeed, not many present-day English city children will fully savour what the Psalmist understood. We appropriate our environment. Denim and silk bear social significance for us. We are makers of meaning, and words are not simply signifiers of concrete data: they articulate new meanings. Present-day English appropriates present-day contexts to bring about new meaning adequate to this context.

Eckhart tells us 'God is not good', drawing attention to the inadequacy of our word 'good' to describe the goodness of God. Aquinas tells us all religious language is analogical, part true, part false. The translator stands along the spectrum from fundamentalist conservative to radical modernity. To opt for either end must be to betray the meaning in either language.

Bibliography

Allen, Jr, H. T. (2001), 'Ecumenist Calls Rome's Translation Norms Unrealistic, Authoritarian' in *National Catholic Reporter* (29 June).

Bradshaw, P. F. and Johnson, M. E. (2012), *The Eucharistic Liturgies: Their Evolution and Interpretation* (SPCK, London).

Bugnini, A. (1990), *The Reform of the Liturgy 1948-1975* (The Liturgical Press, Collegeville, MN).

Collins, M. (1990), 'Liturgical Language' in Fink (1990), 651–61.

English Language Liturgical Consultation [ELLC] (1988), *Praying Together: Agreed Liturgical Texts* (Canterbury Press, Norwich).

Fenwick, J. and Spinks, B. (1995), *Worship in Transition: The Twentieth Century Liturgical Movement* (T & T Clark, Edinburgh).

Fink, P. E. (ed.) (1990), *The New Dictionary of Sacramental Worship* (The Liturgical Press, Collegeville, MN).

Hayes, M. A. and Gearon, L. (eds) (1998), *Contemporary Catholic Theology – A Reader* (Gracewing, Leominster).

International Commission on English in the Liturgy [ICEL] (ed.) (1982), *Documents on the Liturgy: 1963–1979: Conciliar, Papal, and Curial Texts* (The Liturgical Press, Collegeville, MN).

International Consultation on English Texts [ICET] (1970 and 1975), *Prayers We Have in Common:Agreed Liturgical Texts* (Fortress Press, Minneapolis, MN).

Jasper, R. C. D. (1989), *The Development of the Anglican Liturgy 1662–1980* (SPCK, London).

Jeffery, P. (2005), *Translating Tradition: A Chant Historian Reads Liturgiam Authenticam* (The Liturgical Press, Collegeville, MN).

Johnson, M. E. (2006), 'Liturgy and Ecumenism: Gifts, Challenges, and Hopes for a Renewed Vision' in *Worship* 80, 2–29.

-(2007), 'The Loss of a Common Language: The End of Ecumenical Liturgical Convergence?' in *Studia Liturgica* 37, 55–72.

Jones, P. (2013), 'From the Editor's Desk' in *New Liturgy* 158–159-160,

8–13.

Kavanagh, A. (1998), 'Liturgy (*Sacrosanctum Concilium*)' in Hayes and Gearon (1998), 445–52.

Krosnicki, Thomas A. (2014), 'Opening rayers for Lent: Forty-four plus One' in *Worship* 88 (2014), 119–36.

Ladrière, J. (1973), 'The Performativity of Liturgical Language' in *Concilium* 9.2, 50–62.

Marini, P. (2007), *A Challenging Reform: Realizing the Vision of the Liturgical Renewal* (The Liturgical Press, Collegeville, MN).

O'Loughlin, T. (2009), 'Liturgical Evolution and the Fallacy of the Continuing Consequence' in *Worship* 83, 312–23.

-(2010), *The Didache: A Window on the Earliest Christians* (SPCK, London).

-(2010a), 'Eucharistic Celebrations: the Chasm between Idea and Reality' in *New Blackfriars* 91, 423–38.

- (2012), 'A Vernacular Liturgy versus a Liturgy in the "Vernacular"?' in *Worship* 86, 244–55.

-(2012a), '*Latina veritas!* – language as a guarantor of truth?' in *The Furrow* 63, 343–7.

- (2013), 'Is every translation a vernacular translation?' in *New Blackfriars* 94, 508–17.

-(2013a), 'Blessing and breaking: a dissonance of action and interpretation in the Eucharistic Prayers of the Roman Rite' in *Anaphora* 7:2, 53–66.

Ong, W. (2002), *Orality and Literacy: The Technologizing of the Word* (Routledge, London).

Rahner, K. and Häussling, A. (1968), *The Celebration of the Eucharist* (Burns and Oates, London).

Searle, M. (2006), *Called to Participate: Theological, Ritual, and Social Perspectives* (The Liturgical Press, Collegeville, MN).

Taylor, M. (2009), *It's the Eucharist, Thank God* (Decani Books, Brandon, Suffolk).

Whelan, T. R. (2008), 'Liturgical Formation: To What End?' in *Anaphora* 2:2, 1–20.

Appendix
Some Illustrative Examples of the
Translations into English of 1973 and 2011

Vigil of Pentecost: Opening Prayer [Collect]		
1973		2011
Almighty and ever-living God, you fulfilled the Easter promise by sending us your Holy Spirit. May that Spirit unite the races and nations of the earth to proclaim your glory. Grant this through our Lord Jesus Christ, your Son, who lives and reigns with you and the Holy Spirit, one God, for ever and ever.	*Omnipotens sempiterne Deus, qui paschale sacramentum quinquaginta dierum voluisti mysterio ontineri, praesta, ut, gentium facta dispersione, divisiones linguarum ad unam confessionem tui nominis caelesti munere congregentur. Per Dominum nostrum Iesum Christum Filium tuum, qui tecum vivit et regnat in unitate Spiritus Sancti, Deus, per omnia saecula saeculorum.*	Almighty ever-living God, who willed the Paschal Mystery to be encompassed as a sign in fifty days, grant that from out of the scattered nations the confusion of many tongues may be gathered by heavenly grace into one great confession of your name. Through our Lord Jesus Christ, your Son, who lives and reigns with you in the unity of the Holy Spirit, one God, for ever and ever.

Wednesday before the Baptism of the Lord: Opening Prayer [Collect]		
1973		2011
God, light of all nations, give us the joy of lasting peace, and fill us with your radiance as you filled the hearts of our fathers. We ask this through our Lord Jesus Christ, your Son, who lives and reigns with you and the Holy Spirit, one God, for ever and ever.	*Concede nobis, mnipotens Deus, ut salutare tuum, quod ad redemptionem mundi luce nova caelorum processit, nostris semper innovandis cordibus oriatur. Per Dominum nostrum Iesum Christum Filium tuum, qui tecum vivit et regnat in unitate Spiritus Sancti, Deus, per omnia saecula saeculorum.*	Grant us, almighty God, that the bringer of your salvation, who for the world's redemption came forth with newness of heavenly light, may dawn afresh in our hearts and bring us constant renewal. Who lives and reigns with you in the unity of the Holy Spirit, one God, for ever and ever.

Eucharistic Prayer IV – part of the Institution Narrative		
1973		2011
He always loved those who were his own in the world. When the time came for him to be glorified by you, his heavenly Father, he showed the depth of his love. While they were at supper, he took bread, said the blessing, broke the bread,and gave it to his disciples, saying:	*Ipse enim, cum hora venisset ut glorificaretur a te, Pater sancta, ac dilexisset suos qui erant in mundo, in finem dilexit eos: et cenantibus illis accepit panem, benedixit ac fregit, deditque discipulis suis, dicens:*	For when the hour had come for him to be glorified by you, Father most holy, having loved his own who were in the world, he loved them to the end: and while they were at supper, he took bread, blessed and broke it, and gave it to his disciples, saying:

1 On the problems of translating this text, see T. O'Loughlin, 'Blessing and Breaking: A Dissonance of Action and Interpretation in the Eucharistic Prayers of the Roman Rite', *Anaphora* 7:2 (2013) 53–66.

Eucharistic Prayer I – Commemoration of the Living (part of)[2]		
1973		2011
Remember, Lord, your people, Especially those for whom we now pray, *n*. and *n*.. Remember all of us who are gathered here before you and dedicate ourselves to you. We offer you this sacrifice of praise For ourselves and those who are dear to us…	*Memento, Domine, famulorum famularumque tuarum n. et n. et omnium circumstantium, quorum tibi fides cognita est et nota devotio, pro quibus tibi offerimus: vel qui tibi offerunt hoc sacrificum laudis, pro se suisque omnibus:…*	Remember, Lord, your servants *n*. and *n*. and all gathered here, whose faith and devotion are known to you. For them, we offer you this sacrifice of praise or they offer it for themselves and all who are dear to them:…

---

2 That the Latin text is corrupt in this prayer was first pointed out in 1903 by Edmund Bishop (in JTS 4(1903) 555–77), see his Liturgica Historica (Oxford 1918), 95. The 2011 translation has managed to translate a non-sentence as if it were a sentence.